Sorting

Peter Patilla

Heinemann
LIBRARY

First published in Great Britain by Heinemann Library,
Halley Court, Jordan Hill, Oxford OX2 8EJ,
a division of Reed Educational and Professional Publishing Ltd.
Heinemann is a registered trademark of Reed Educational & Professional Publishing Limited.

OXFORD MELBOURNE AUCKLAND
JOHANNESBURG BLANTYRE GABORONE
IBADAN PORTSMOUTH NH (USA) CHICAGO

Designed by AMR
Illustrations by Jessica Stockam (Beehive Illustration)
Originated by HBM Print Ltd, Singapore
Printed and bound by South China Printing Co., Hong Kong/China

03 02 01 00 99
10 9 8 7 6 5 4 3 2 1

ISBN 0 431 093547

British Library Cataloguing in Publication Data
Patilla, Peter
  Sorting. – (Maths links)
  1.Geometrical constructions – Juvenile literature
  I.Title.
  516.1·5

Acknowledgements
The Publishers would like to thank the following for permission to reproduce photographs:
Trevor Clifford, pgs 4, 5, 6, 8, 9, 10, 11, 12, 13, 15, 16, 17, 19, 20, 21, 23, 28; Oxford Scientific Films, pg 25 (t) /David B. Fleetham; Tony Stone Images, pg 25 (b) /Val Corbett.

Cover photograph reproduced with permission of Trevor Clifford.

Our thanks to David Kirkby for his comments in the preparation of this book.

Every effort has been made to contact copyright holders of any material reproduced in this book. Any omissions will be rectified in subsequent printings if notice is given to the Publisher.

For more information about Heinemann Library books, or to order, please phone +44 (0)1865 888066, or send a fax to +44 (0)1865 314091. You can visit our website at www.heinemann.co.uk

Contents

Some words are shown in bold, **like this**. You can find out what they mean by looking in the Glossary.

Matching pairs

Sometimes things go in **pairs**. The pair may be
exactly the same, or very nearly the same. Some
pairs have a left and right.

We often have to sort out **matching** pairs. It would be strange to wear socks which did not match.

Can you find the matching pairs of socks in the picture? How many pairs are there?

Partners

We often **match** pairs which go together. Both pieces are needed to make something work. Having a video recorder without a tape is not much fun.

We match pairs of things for lots of reasons.

For example, we match shapes, sizes or colours.

Look at the picture and find matching pairs.
Why do they go together?

Sorting by use

When starting a **task**, we need to **collect** all the items we might need to use. It is very annoying to forget something important. Always check you have everything before starting.

We use all sorts of things when we are working or playing.

Look at the picture and sort out what this girl needs to go swimming. Can you think of anything else she might need?

Odd one out

Sometimes when we sort things, there is an odd one out. Something might be a slightly different size, shape or colour. Spotting the odd one out can be important.

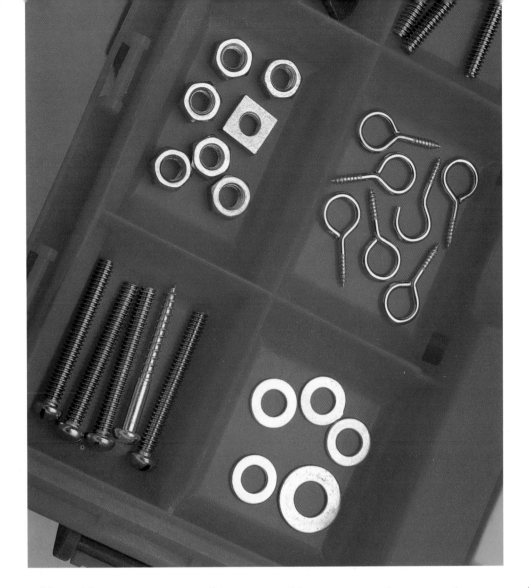

In **collections**, it is often quite easy to spot an odd one out.

Look at the sorting in the picture. Can you spot the odd ones out?

Colour sorting

When we sort for colour, the colours are not always the same **shade**. We use words such as dark, bright, light and deep to describe shades of colour.

12

We can use shades of colour when making patterns.

Look at the picture. Which colours does the girl need to finish the pattern? The shade of colour is important.

Shape sorting

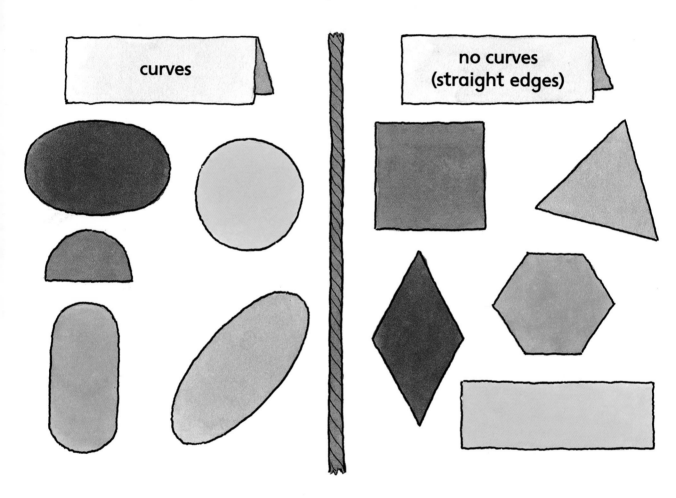

Here is a **diagram** for sorting shapes. We sort shapes for many reasons. This diagram sorts into shapes with curves, and shapes with straight edges.

14

pieces without straight edges

Jigsaw pieces can be sorted by shape.

The picture shows shapes being sorted. The reason for sorting is to find pieces with straight edges. Pieces with straight edges go into the box. Others are left outside.

Look at the unsorted pieces. How many can you find that should go in the box?

Subsets

A set can sometimes be sorted into smaller sets called **subsets**. A set of farm animals can be sorted into subsets of ducks, cows, sheep and horses. Finding subsets can be useful.

We sometimes use subsets when we tidy up.

In the picture the boy is tidying knives, forks and spoons into subsets. How many in each subset still need sorting?

Re-sorting

hooves

no hooves

four legs

does not have four legs

Sorting can often be done in more than one way. A set can be sorted for lots of different reasons, such as colour, shape and size. These farm animals have been sorted in two different ways.

18

When playing games, we often sort for different reasons. You can sort dominoes for reasons such as: 'has a **blank**', or 'has an **even number** of spots'.

Can you think of some more ways of sorting dominoes?

Two reasons for sorting

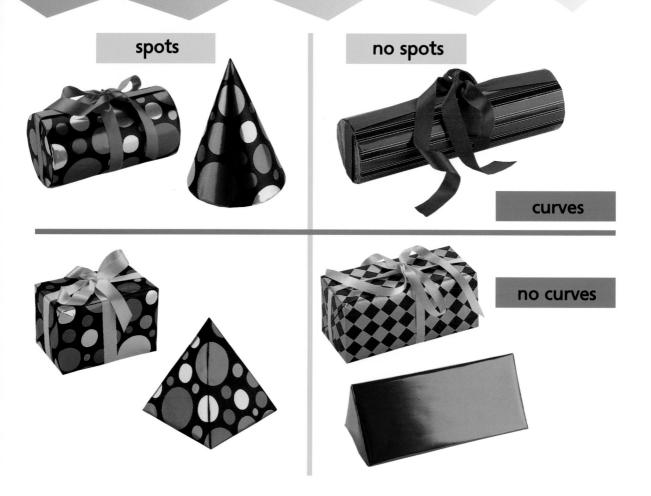

spots	no spots
	curves
	no curves

We can sort for two reasons. We may want to choose presents that are spotted and have curves. This diagram shows presents sorted for those two reasons.

This **diagram** shows sorting for shape and colour.

Can you find any more shapes that belong where the two hoops cross over? Can you find shapes to fit in the other parts of the hoops?

Complete sets

Some sets have to be complete. If something is missing it will spoil the set. A jigsaw with one piece missing spoils the puzzle.

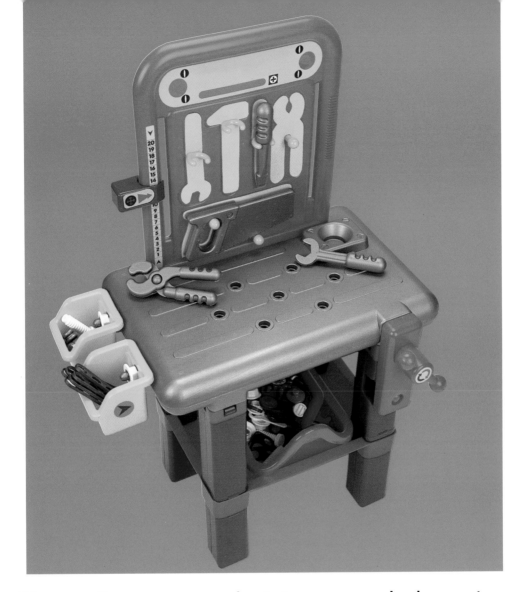

Outlines, **diagrams** and pictures can help us to see whether something is missing from a set.

Look at the the picture. What do you think is missing from the set?

23

Family sets

Sometimes things in a set belong to a family. They may not look exactly the same, but they have a family likeness. Here is a family of **rectangles**.

shoal of fish

flock of sheep

Some sets of animals have special names, such as a **pack** of wolves or a **flock** of birds.

Do you know any other special names for family sets of animals?

Charts and diagrams

Alex   Lucy   Mark   Anna   Maria

Drawing a **chart** can make finding information easier. From the height chart you can see who is tallest and who is shortest. You can also see which children are about the same height.

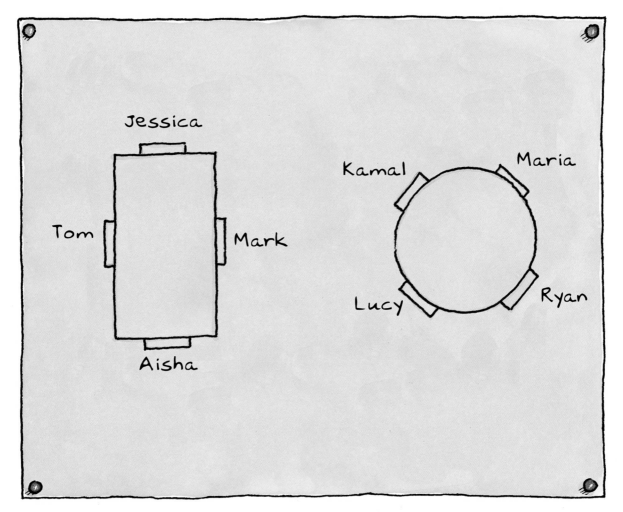

a seating plan

Charts and **diagrams** can be used to **organize** things. They can sort out where things go, or where people sit.

Look at the picture. Who is sitting next to Maria?

Tables

	rolls	sandwiches	biscuits	fruit	drinks
Aisha	I		I	I	I
Jessica		I		I	I
Kamal		I	I	I	I
Lucy	I			I	I
Maria	I		I		I
Mark		I	I	I	I
Ryan	I	I	I	I	I
Tom		I	I	I	I
Total	IIII	ⅢⅢ	ⅢⅢ I	ⅢⅢ II	ⅢⅢ III

This table shows what 8 children want in their lunch boxes.

When we sort things, we sometimes write them in a **table** with **rows** across and **columns** down. **Tally marks** are ticks, drawn to show the number of things. The tally mark for 5 is ⅢⅢ.

Monday	Tuesday	Wednesday	Thursday	Friday	Saturday	Sunday
			1 swimming	2	3	4 visit Gran
5	6	7	8 swimming	9	10	11
12	13	14	15 swimming	16	17 Lucy's party	18
19	20	21	22 swimming	23	24	25
26 my birthday	27	28	29	30 go to dentist	31	

We can use tables to help us remember things.
A monthly planner is a kind of table called a
calendar.

Look at the planner. When is the party? Why not
make your own monthly planner?

Glossary

blank empty. In dominoes, a blank has no spots.

calendar shows each month of the year and how many days are in each month

chart a place to write down information

collection sets of things

column the up and down section of a chart or diagram

diagram a simple plan used to show something

even numbers numbers of things that can be put into twos exactly without any left over. 2, 4, 6, 8, 10 are even numbers.

flock a set of birds or sheep

matching things that are the same as each other

organize to tidy something up

pack a set. People talk about a pack of cards, a pack of dogs and a pack of lies.

pair a pair is two things

rectangle 4-sided shape with no curves

row the across section of a table, chart or diagram

shade a colour shade is how dark or light the colour is

subsets parts of a larger set. A set of children has two subsets – boys and girls.

table something you sit at, or a chart or diagram. This often has rows and columns.

tally marks made to show how many are in a set or group. They are little lines, like sticks. Sometimes they are put into sets of five like this ⑅.

task a job or piece of work

Answers

Index